SMALLWOOD'S PIANO TUTOR

JOHN WOOD ENG.

FRANCIS, DAY & HUNTER Ltd.

© 2006 by Faber Music Ltd
First published by International Music Publications Ltd
International Music Publications Ltd is a Faber Music company
Bloomsbury House 74–77 Great Russell Street London WC1B 3DA
Printed in England by Caligraving Ltd
All rights reserved

ISBN10: 0-571-52768-X
EAN13: 978-0-571-52768-7

To buy Faber Music publications or to find out about the full range of titles available,
please contact your local music retailer or Faber Music sales enquiries:

Faber Music Ltd, Burnt Mill, Elizabeth Way, Harlow, CM20 2HX England
Tel: +44(0)1279 82 89 82   Fax: +44(0)1279 82 89 83
sales@fabermusic.com   fabermusic.com

CONTENTS

William Smallwood's Pianoforte Tutor

Musical sounds are explained by characters called notes, which are named after the first seven letters of the alphabet, namely, A. B. C. D. E. F. G.   The notes are written upon what is termed the Stave.
The Stave consists of five lines and four spaces which run parallel across the book, thus:-

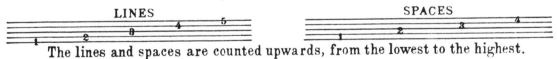

The lines and spaces are counted upwards, from the lowest to the highest.

The names of the notes are determined by the Clef which is placed at the commencement of the stave. There are various Clefs, but only two are necessary for the Pianoforte: the Treble or G Clef, which is placed on the second line of the stave: and the Bass or F Clef, which is placed on the fourth line of the stave:

Two staves are required, as a rule, for Pianoforte music; they are joined together by a Brace, thus:-

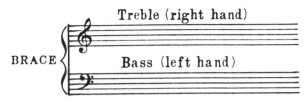

NAMES OF THE TREBLE NOTES

E is on the 1st line, G is on the 2nd line, B is on the 3rd line, D is on the 4th line, F is on the 5th line.
F is in the 1st space,   A is in the 2nd space, C is in the 3rd space,   E is in the 4th space.

The stave is enlarged by added lines, called Ledger lines, and two notes can be obtained by having one below the stave and another above it:-      Ledger lines below the stave

which can be carried further if desired.

C is upon the 1st ledger line below the Treble stave, B is below the 1st ledger line below the Treble stave,
A is upon the 2nd ledger line below the Treble stave, G is below the 2nd ledger line below the Treble stave,
F is upon the 3rd ledger line below the Treble stave.

Ledger lines above the Treble stave

A is upon the 1st ledger line above the Treble stave, B is above the 1st ledger line above the Treble stave,
C is upon the 2nd ledger line above the Treble stave, D is above the 2nd ledger line above the Treble stave,
E is upon the 3rd ledger line above the Treble stave, F is above the 3rd ledger line above the Treble stave,
G is upon the 4th ledger line above the Treble stave.

It is better not to learn the ledger lines until the notes on the stave are conquered.

2

As soon as the pupil has learned the following, so that they are known on the book at once, several of the little excercises can be practised after learning the names of the Keys of the Pianoforte.

The pupil should learn the Treble notes before attempting the Bass.

NAMES OF THE BASS NOTES

G is on the 1st line,   B is on the 2nd line,   D is on the 3rd line,   F is on the 4th line,   A is on the 5th line.
A is in the 1st space,   C is in the 2nd space,   E is in the 3rd space,   G is in the 4th space.

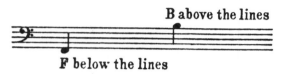

E is upon the 1st ledger line below the Bass stave,   D is below the 1st ledger line below the Bass stave,
C is upon the 2nd ledger line below the Bass stave,   B is below the 2nd ledger line below the Bass stave,
A is upon the 3rd ledger line below the Bass stave.

C is upon the 1st ledger line above the Bass stave,   D is above the 1st ledger line above the Bass stave,
E is upon the 2nd ledger line above the Bass stave,   F is above the 2nd ledger line above the Bass stave,
G is upon the 3rd ledger line above the Bass stave.

The remarks (see top of page) in regard to learning the Treble notes apply equally to the Bass,   and the pupil is advised to master thoroughly the following as soon as possible.

THE DIFFERENT KINDS OF NOTES, THEIR VALUE, &c., &c.,

In modern music there are six different kinds of notes, viz: the Semibreve, Minim, Crotchet, Quaver, Semiquaver and the Demisemiquaver.

The Semibreve is a round open note o, the Minim is a round open note with a stem ♩, the Crotchet is a black note with a stem ♩, the Quaver is a black note with a stem and tail ♪, the Semiquaver is a black note with a stem and two tails ♬ and the Demisemiquaver is a black note with a stem and three tails ♬

Each note has its corresponding rest, which is equal in duration to the note it represents.

2

F. & D. Ltd. 1079-8627

| Semibreve rest | Minim rest | Crotchet rest | Quaver rest | Semiquaver rest | Demisemiquaver rest |

The Semibreve rest is placed under a line of the stave, the Minim rest on a line of the stave. There are two forms of the Crotchet rest, as shown above. The Quaver rest turns to the left, the Semiquaver rest with two hooks turns to the left and the Demisemiquaver rest with three hooks turns to the left.

The proportion which these notes bear to each other is as follows:
One Semibreve is equal to two Minims, one Minim is equal to two Crotchets, one Crotchet is equal to two Quavers, one Quaver is equal to two Semiquavers and one Semiquaver is equal to two Demisemiquavers.
The same proportion also applies to the rests.

One Semibreve is therefore equal to 2 minims or 4 crotchets or 8 quavers or 16 semiquavers or 32 demisemiquavers. One Minim is equal to 2 crotchets or 4 quavers or 8 semiquavers or 16 demisemiquavers. One Crotchet is equal to 2 quavers or 4 semiquavers or 8 demisemiquavers. One Quaver is equal to 2 semiquavers or 4 demisemiquavers. One Semiquaver is equal to 2 demisemiquavers.

TABLE
A Semibreve

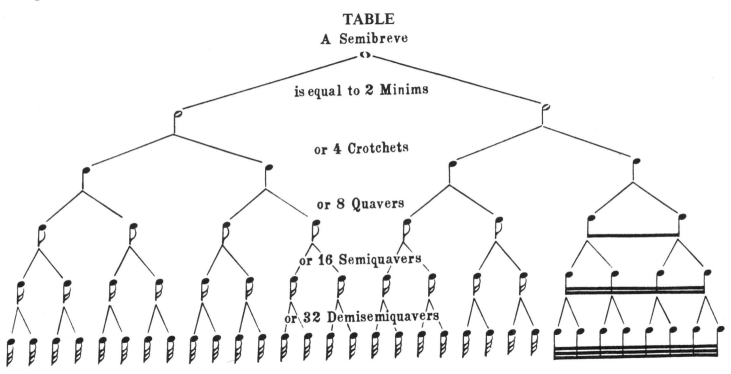

is equal to 2 Minims

or 4 Crotchets

or 8 Quavers

or 16 Semiquavers

or 32 Demisemiquavers

A dot after a note makes it half as long again: for instance, a dotted Semibreve is equal to 3 Minims, a dotted Minim to 3 Crotchets, and so on; see example below.

a dotted Semibreve	a dotted Minim	a dotted Crotchet	a dotted Quaver	a dotted Semiquaver
is equal to 3 Minims	is equal to 3 Crotchets	is equal to 3 Quavers	is equal to 3 Semiquavers	is equal to 3 Demisemiquavers

Sometimes Notes are double dotted, that is, have two dots after them; in this case the notes are increased three fourths of their original value.

The above remarks apply exactly the same respecting rests; therefore, the dots increase the duration of the rests in the same proportion that they do to notes.

F. & D. Ltd. 1079 - 8627

ON TIME

Bars are short upright lines drawn through the stave, which divide the music into equal portions of time. Double bars divide the music into strains or parts.

The Semibreve is considered the Standard note by which the measure of the different species of time is fixed.

The time signatures are placed at the beginning of a piece.

Simple Common Time

 stands for Common time with the value of a semibreve in each bar.

 indicates two fourths of a semibreve in each bar — *two Crotchets.*

Simple Triple Time

 indicates three quarters of a semibreve in each bar—*three Crotchets.*

indicates three eights of a semibreve in each bar — *three Quavers.*

The above examples are *Simple Time.* In all cases where the upper figure is less than 6 it is *Simple Time,* but when the upper figure is 6 or more than 6 it is *Compound Time.* There are then in use the following different kinds of time, viz:

Simple Common Time and *Compound Common Time; Simple Triple Time* and *Compound Triple Time.*

Compound Common Time

indicates that there are 6 of the eight quavers which make a semibreve in each bar

twelve quavers in a bar.

There is only one species of Compound Triple Time in general use and that is—

or nine quavers in a bar.

To know whether a piece is in Common or Triple time, it will be necessary to observe that when the top figure is *even*, it is *Common Time*, if *odd* it is *Triple Time*; also, if the upper figure is less than 6 it is *Simple Time*, but if 6 or more it is *Compound Time.*

PIANOFORTE KEYBOARD

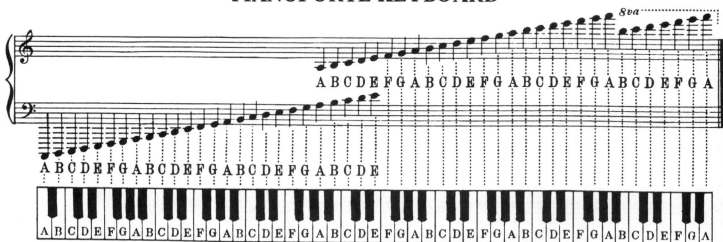

On examining the Key board of the Pianoforte it will be observed that there are White and Black Keys; the former represent the natural notes, and the latter the flats and sharps. The Black Keys are divided into alternate groups of two and three, and considering this, the names of the White Keys are readily known. To make this very easy to remember,

D is between the two black keys;
E is on the right of the two black keys;
F is on the left of the three black keys;
G is above the lowest of the three black keys;
A is above the middle one of the three black keys;
B is on the right of the three black keys;
C is on the left of the two black keys.

PREPARATORY LESSONS

1 stands for the thumb — 2 for the first finger — 3 second finger — 4 third finger — 5 fourth finger
This page is in Common Time of 4 crotchets in each bar

RIGHT HAND ONLY

Take care not to count the semibreve at the end of each exercise too quickly.

F.& D. Ltd. 1079 - 8627

PREPARATORY LESSONS (continued)

BOTH HANDS

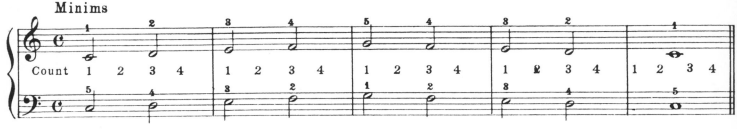

Slow and even counting is essential.

Endeavour to maintain strict time in all exercises.

Correct fingering as shown must be used to ensure smooth playing.

Begin these exercises slowly and gradually increase speed. *Don't* memorise the sound, but *read* every note and play it as written with its correct time value.

PREPARATORY LESSONS (continued)

Common time — four quavers in a bar.

Chord

Chord

WALTZ. Triple time — three crotchets in a bar.

Chord

*The dots at the double bar signify that the parts are to be repeated.
These exercises must be carefully counted during practice, as they show the different kinds of time in common use.

F.& D. Ltd. 1079 - 8627

PREPARATORY LESSONS (continued)

Common Time — four crotchets in a bar

Common Time — four quavers in a bar

Triple Time — three crotchets in a bar

DAILY EXERCISES
To be played slowly at first, with increase of time as the pupil improves.

PRELUDES, LESSONS, FAVOURITE AIRS, &c., in Familiar Keys
PRELUDE, KEY OF C

FAVOURITE REEL

*When the figure 3 is placed over a group of three notes, it indicates a Triplet; that is, three notes are played in the time of two of the same species.

†Various Italian Terms are used to signify the speed of the different pieces; refer to the list at the end of the book.

f stands for Forte—loud; p for Piano—soft; pp for Pianissimo — very soft.

F. & D. Ltd. 1079 - 8627

SLOW AIR

MARCH

The Scale of C running two octaves should now be practised from the table of Scales at the end of the book (*page 50*).

F. & D. Ltd. 1079 - 8627

12

HUNGARIAN MELODY

EXTENSIONS

PRELUDE

WALTZ

POLKA

*When a piece commences with only a portion of a bar (as in this instance), the last bar of the strain must contain only as much as is wanting to make it complete at the beginning.
Da Capo, or *D.C.*, means go back to the beginning of the piece. Finish where the word *Fine* is placed.

F. & D. Ltd. 1079 - 8627

QUICK MARCH

Moderato

BEAMS OF MORNING

Moderato

SCALE IN CONTRARY MOTION

† *8va*

*The curve over the notes signifies that they have to be played smoothly from one note to another.
† *8va* signifies that the notes are to be played an octave higher than written.
The Scale in contrary motion should be practised over and over again playing the last note (the semibreve) only when finishing.

It will now be necessary to notice the different characters termed Sharps, Flats and Naturals.

On the Pianoforte each Black key has two names; for instance, the black key between C and D is C sharp and D flat; the black key between D and E is D sharp and E flat; and so on.

The sharp (♯) raises the note before which it is placed a semitone, which is the next black key to the right.

The flat (♭) lowers the note a semitone, which is the next black key to the left.

The natural (♮) restores to its original state any note that has been altered by a sharp or flat.

It will be observed that there is no black key between E and F, and between B and C. When E♯ is wanted it will of course, have to be played on the white key to the right, and F♭ on the white key to the left. These latter, however, the student will not require for some time to come, as they only occur in extreme keys.

When sharps or flats are placed immediately after the clefs at the commencement of a piece they signify that all the notes of the *same name* are to be played sharp or flat *throughout the piece*, or so far as a change of key, which would be indicated.

Accidental sharps, flats, or naturals which are inserted before notes in the course of a piece only effect those before which they are placed, or throughout the bar in which they occur.

KEY OF G
The Key of G requires one sharp: F♯
PRELUDE

YOUTHFUL DAYS

WHEN I REMEMBER

The *Crescendo* ———— signifies a gradual increase in the tone, and the
Diminuendo ———— just the contrary.

F. & D. Ltd. 1079 - 8627

HOME

THE BLUE BELLS OF SCOTLAND

Practise now the Scale of G from the Table at the end of the book (*page 50*)

WON'T YOU BUY MY PRETTY FLOWERS

G. W. PERSLEY

Heed - less of the night winds bit - ter As they round a - bout her whirl.
Heed - less of the tear - drops gleaming In her sad and wist - ful eye.

While the hun - dreds pass un - heed - ing In the ev - 'ning's wan - ing hours.
How her lit - tle heart is sigh - ing In the cold and drea - ry hours!

Still she cries with tear - ful plead - ing "Won't you buy my pret - ty flowers?"
On - ly lis - ten to her cry - ing "Won't you buy my pret - ty flowers?"

There are ma - ny sad and wea - ry, In this pleasant world of ours

Cry - ing ev - 'ry night so drea - ry, "Won't you buy my pret - ty flowers?"

D.C.

SCALE IN CONTRARY MOTION

F. & D. Ltd. 1079 - 8627

KEY OF D

The Key of D requires two sharps; F♯ and C♯

PRELUDE

BOHEMIAN MELODY

Practise the Scale of D at the end of the book (*page 50*)

FAIRY DANCE

*The tie over two notes which are the same signifies that the second is not to be played but held down the length of the two.

F. & D. Ltd. 1079-8627

SWISS GALOP

SCALE IN CONTRARY MOTION

F. & D. Ltd. 1079 - 8627

KEY OF A
The Key of A requires three sharps; F♯, C♯ and G♯
PRELUDE

SWEETLY FLOWING

Repeat the Treble 8va higher

Repeat the Treble 8va higher

AIR – IN LUCIA DI LAMMERMOOR

DONIZETTI

Practise the Scale of A at the end of the book (*page 51*)

SCALE IN CONTRARY MOTION

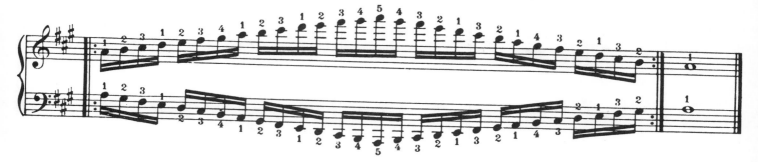

KEY OF E

The Key of E requires four sharps; F♯, C♯, G♯ and D♯

PRELUDE

KIND WORDS

HUNGARIAN WALTZ

Practise the Scale of E at the end of the book (*page 51*)

SCALE IN CONTRARY MOTION

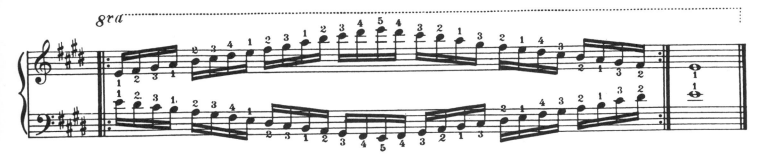

*The dotted minim in the bass of each bar is struck as the first note, and then held down during the whole bar.

F. & D. Ltd. 1079-8627

KEY OF F

The Key of F requires one flat; B♭

PRELUDE

CARNIVAL OF VENICE

Practise the Scale of F at the end of the book (*page 52*)

MERRY CHRISTMAS MAZURKA

F. & D. Ltd. 1079-8627

AULD LANG SYNE

SCALE IN CONTRARY MOTION

COMPLIN CHIMES – ST. PETER'S, ROME

ST. PATRICK'S GUILD MARCH

KEY OF B FLAT

The Key of B flat requires two flats; B♭ and E♭

PRELUDE

BAY OF DUBLIN — (Valsette)

Practise the Scale of B♭ at the end of the book (*page 52*)

SCALE IN CONTRARY MOTION

F. & D. Ltd. 1079 - 8627

KEY OF E FLAT

The Key of E flat requires three flats; B♭, E♭ and A♭

PRELUDE

Practise the Scale of E♭ at the end of the book (*page 52*)

AIR from LA SONNAMBULA

BELLINI

SCALE IN CONTRARY MOTION

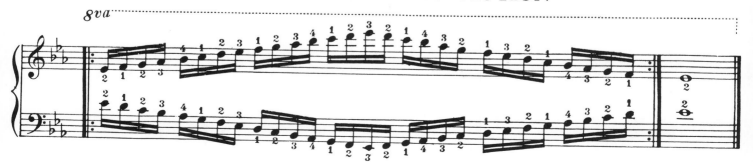

KEY OF A FLAT

The Key of A flat requires four flats; Bb, Eb, Ab and Db

PRELUDE

MELODY

Practise the Scale of Ab at the end of the book (*page 53*)

D.C. al Fine

SCALE IN CONTRARY MOTION

SILVER THREADS AMONG THE GOLD

Composed by H. P. DANKS,
Arr. by Wᵐ SMALLWOOD

THE DIATONIC SCALE OR SCALE OF NATURE

The Diatonic Scale consists of five whole tones and two semitones; the semitones occur in the Major mode:

In ascending between the 3rd and 4th and between the 7th and 8th degrees of the Scale thus:—

In descending between the 8th and 7th, and the 4th and 3rd thus:—

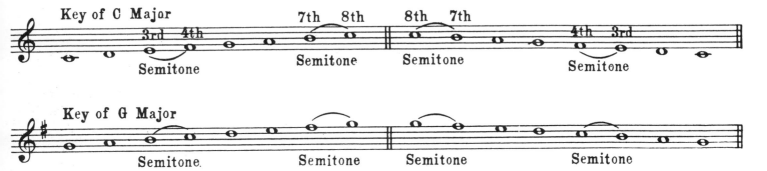

THE MINOR SCALE

The Minor Scale differs from the Major in the position of the semitones, also the descending minor scale is different from the ascending. The semitones occur in ascending between the 2nd and 3rd, and between the 7th and 8th degrees of the scale, and the 6th is raised a semitone also. In descending, the 7th and 6th are flattened a semitone, and the semitones occur between the 6th and 5th, and the 3rd and 2nd.

The Minor Scales and Keys have the same signatures as the relative Majors; the Minor Key being a minor third below the Major Key.

The relative minor of C Major is A Minor

of G Major is E Minor

of D Major is B Minor

of A Major is F♯ Minor

of E Major is C♯ Minor

The relative minor of F Major is D Minor

of B♭ Major is G Minor

of E♭ Major is C Minor

of A♭ Major is F Minor

&c. &c.

SABBATH MELODIES

TO CELEBRATE THY PRAISE, O LORD

To cel - e - brate Thy praise, O Lord, I will my heart pre - pare, To
The thought of them shall to my soul Ex - alt - ed plea - sure bring, Whilst

all the list' - ning world Thy works, Thy won - d'rous works de - clare.
to Thy name, O Thou most High, Tri - um - phant praise I sing.

D.C.

SUN OF MY SOUL, THOU SAVIOUR DEAR.

Sun of my soul, Thou Sa - viour dear, It is not night if Thou be near.

Oh, may no earth - born cloud a - rise To hide Thee from Thy ser - vant's eyes.

OFT IN SORROW, OFT IN WOE

Oft in sor - row, oft in woe, On - ward, Chris - tian, on - ward go,

Fight the fight, main - tain the strife, Strength - ened with the bread of life.

The complete words of the hymns may be found in any of the popular hymn books.

F. & D. Ltd. 1079 - 8627

SABBATH MELODIES

THROUGH ALL THE CHANGING SCENES OF LIFE

"HAMPSTEAD" – SWEET IS THE WORK, MY GOD, MY KING

Wᵐ SMALLWOOD

PARISIAN MELODY – CHILDREN OF THE HEAVENLY KING

Adapted by Wᵐ SMALLWOOD

F. & D. Ltd. 1079 - 8627

SABBATH MELODIES

INDIAN MELODY – THERE IS A HAPPY LAND

There is a | hap-py land | Far far a- | way, | Where saints in | glo-ry stand | Bright, bright as | day.
Bright in that | hap-py land | Beams ev-'ry | eye; | Kept by a | Fa-ther's hand, | Love can-not | die.

O, how they | sweet-ly sing, | Wor-thy is our | Sa-viour King, | Loud let His | prais-es ring, | Praise, praise for | aye.
On, then, to | glo-ry run, | Be a crown and | King-dom won, | And bright a- | bove the sun, | Reign, reign for | aye.

D.C.

FAVOURITE CHANTS

SINGLE CHANT   TALLIS

SINGLE CHANT   FARRANT

SINGLE CHANT   W. RIDLEY

SINGLE CHANT   PURCELL

SINGLE CHANT   A.T. TURNER
(of Ballarat)

SINGLE CHANT   PURCELL

GRAND CHANT   PELHAM HUMPHREYS

SINGLE CHANT   Wm SMALLWOOD

FAVOURITE CHANTS

SABBATH MELODIES
THY WILL BE DONE

Moderato

My God, my Fa - ther, while I stray | Far from my home, on lifes rough way

O teach me from my heart to say, | Thy will be done, Thy wi'l be done.

CUJUS ANIMAM — (STABAT MATER)

ROSSINI

Moderato

SABBATH MELODIES

ONWARD, CHRISTIAN SOLDIERS

NEARER MY GOD, TO THEE

W.m SMALLWOOD

36

DUETTINO – SWEET SMILES

DUETTINO – FAIRY WALTZ

DUETTINO – SWEET SMILES

DUETTINO – FAIRY WALTZ

DUET – MARCH AROUND THE MAY POLE

SECONDO
Moderato

DUET — MARCH AROUND THE MAY POLE

WOODLAND REVELS

GAVOTTE

41

TRIO

NEW   EDINBRO' SCHOTTISCHE

NEW KILLARNEY POLKA

44 INTRODUCTIONS, OR CADENCES, IN VARIOUS KEYS
MAJOR AND MINOR

LESSON

Moderato

Fine

D.C.

CLASSICAL MELODIES
ROMANZA

STEIBELT

MELODY IN F

MOZART

These Classical Melodies may be given with any of the other lessons, at the discretion of the Teacher. They will be found to be excellent practice.

F. & D. Ltd. 1079 - 8627

EARLY DAWN

Wm SMALLWOOD

F. & D. Ltd. 1079 - 8627

D.C. al Fine

CLASSICAL MELODIES

RONDO

HAYDN

✱TEMA

Arranged from BEETHOVEN

This beautiful Melody may be sung to the popular missionary hymn, "From Greenland's icy mountains".

F. & D. Ltd. 1079 - 8627

CLASSICAL MELODIES
RONDO

HAYDN

NATIONAL ANTHEM — GOD SAVE THE QUEEN

1 God save our gra - cious Queen, Long live our no - ble Queen, God save the Queen.

Send her vic - to - ri - ous, Hap-py and glo-ri-ous, Long to reign o - ver us, God save the Queen.

2
O Lord our God arise,
Scatter her enemies,
    And make them fall.
Confound their politics,
Frustrate their knavish tricks,
On thee our hopes we fix,
    God save the Queen.

3
Thy choicest gifts in store,
On her be pleased to pour,
    Long may she reign.
May she defend our laws,
And ever give us cause
To sing with heart and voice,
    God save the Queen.

F. & D. Ltd. 1079 - 8627

GRACES OR NOTES OF EMBELLISHMENT

The most important Graces in music are the Appoggiatura, the Turn and the Shake.

The Appoggiatura is expressed by a small-sized note, placed before the principal note. It borrows one-half the value of the principal note, unless that note is dotted, in which case the appoggiatura borrows two-thirds of it

Written thus:

If the small note has a dash drawn through it thus: ♪ it is played *smartly, quickly.*

Played thus:

The Turn, (∾, or ⁊) consists of a principal note and the notes above and below; it should be played with decision.

Written thus:

Turn upon the note. Inverted Turn. Turn with a sharp. Turn with a flat. Turn over a note

Played thus:

The (*tr*) is a rapid alternate repetition of the principal note and the note above. It generally ends with a turn.

Written thus:

Commencing with the principal note   Commencing with the note above

Played thus:

The Transient or Short Shake
Written thus:

Of the Tremando
Written thus:

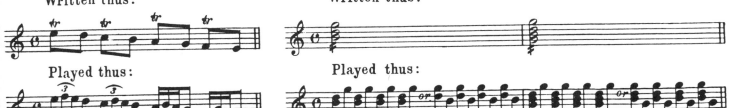

Played thus: Played thus:

The Waved line, thus { or the Curved line, thus (when placed before a chord, signifies that the notes are to be played in the Arpeggio style, that is, to commence with the lowest note of the chord, and proceed in a quick and regular succession, keeping each note down when struck

Played thus:

SCALES

The Scales must be practised slowly at first, then more quickly by degrees as the pupil improves.
The hands may be practised separately at the commencement.
The careful practice of the Scales is of the greatest possible importance.

Be particular to observe where the thumb is to be placed.

F.& D. Ltd. 1079-8627

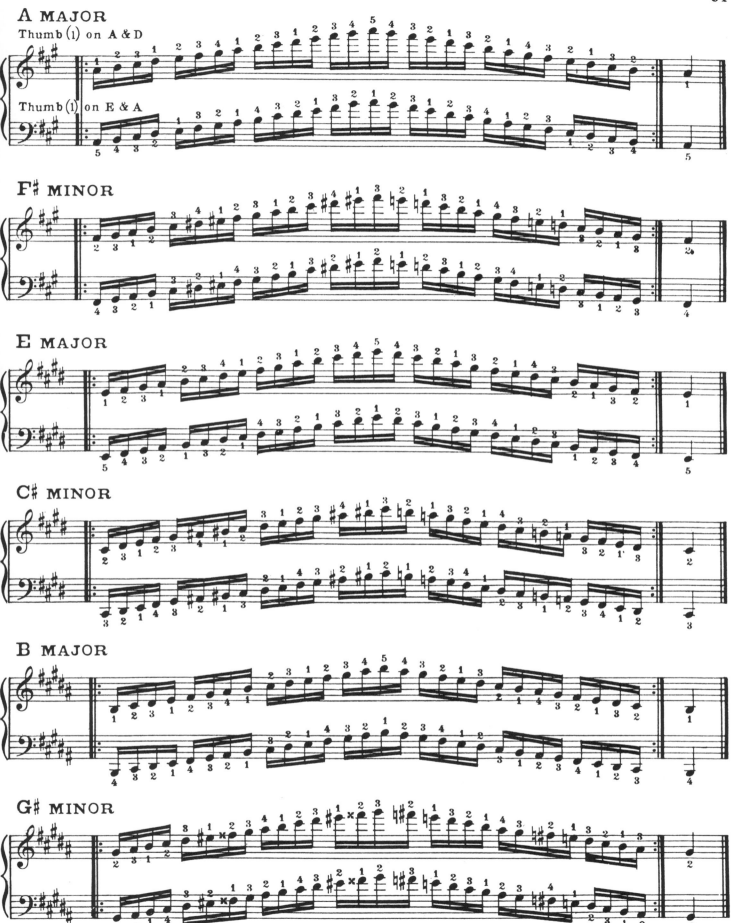

F MAJOR

D MINOR

B♭ MAJOR

G MINOR

E♭ MAJOR

C MINOR

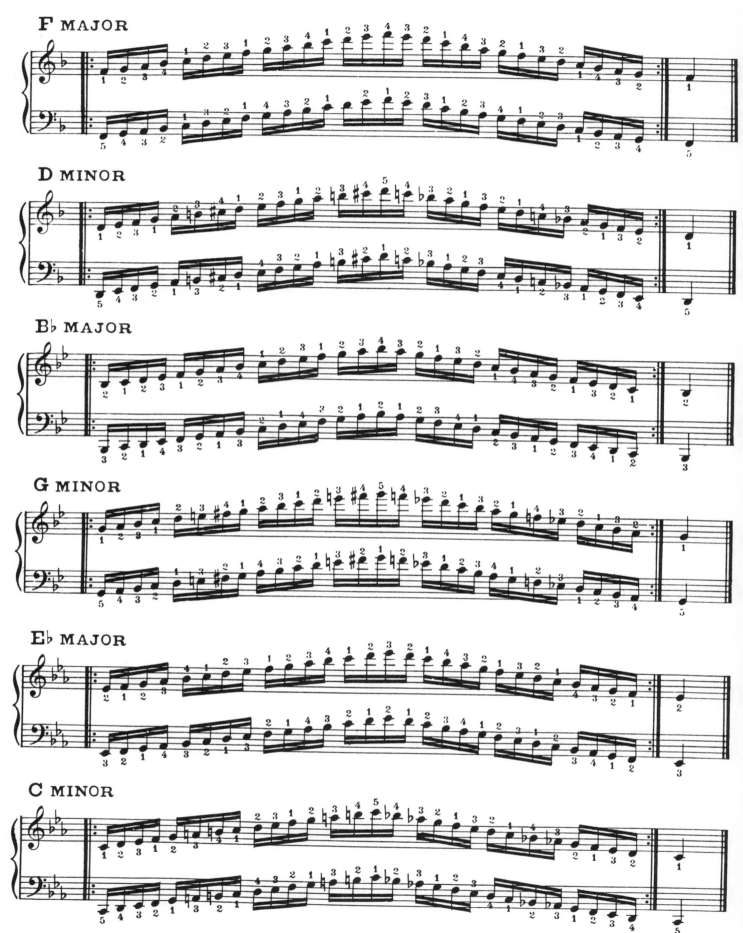

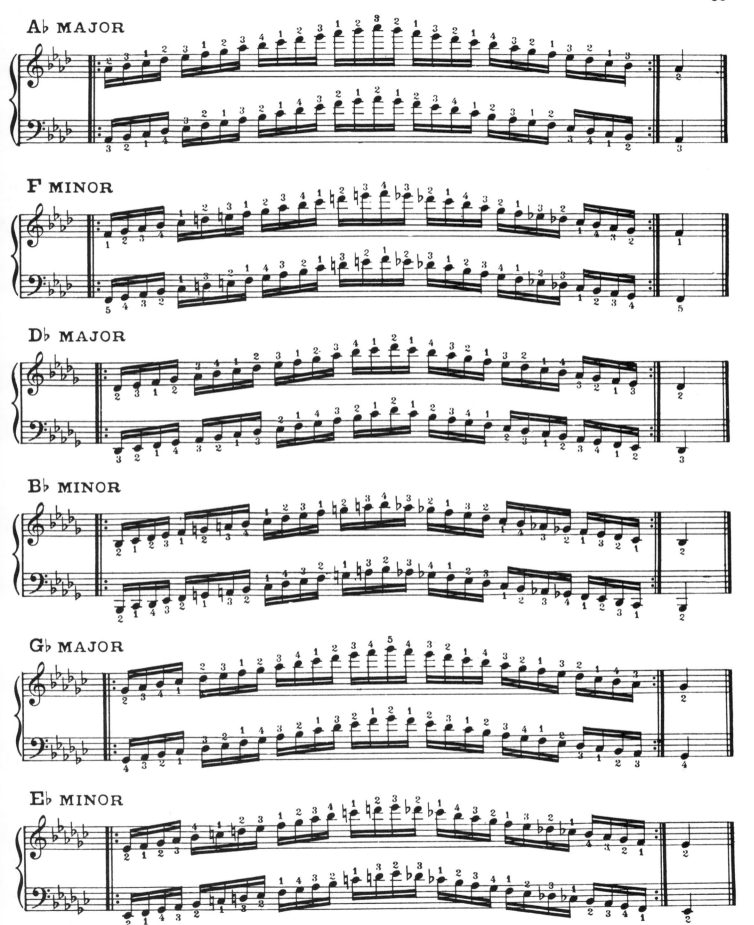

CHROMATIC SCALE

A FEW QUESTIONS WITH THEIR ANSWERS
ON THE THEORY OF MUSIC

Q What is an octave?

A An eighth.

Q What are English terms for the notes which form an octave?

A The key note is called the Tonic; the 2nd above, the Supertonic; the 3rd above, the Mediant; the 4th above, the Subdominant; the 5th above, the Dominant; the 6th above, the Submediant; the 7th above, the Leading note; the 8th above, the Octave.

Q What is Modulation?

A A change of Key.

Q What is the difference between gradual and abrupt Modulation?

A Gradual Modulation is a change into some Key which is the nearest and most natural to the one in which the composition is written, while abrupt Modulation is a change into some distant Key.

Q What is a partial Modulation?

A A change of key which is no sooner made than it returns at once to the original.

Q What is Transposition?

A The art of removing a composition into a higher or lower key, so as to be better adapted to some particular voice or instrument.

Q What is Melody?

A A succession of single notes or sounds.

Q What is Harmony?

A Two or more sounds heard at the same time in proper order.

Q What does a Common Chord consist of?

A A bass note with its 3rd and 5th, the octave to the bass being generally added.

Q What are the attendant Harmonies to the chord of the Tonic?

A The Chords of the Subdominant and Dominant.

Q How many sounds does the chord of the Dominant 7th consist of?

A Four, the chord of the Dominant and its 7th added, the 7th being a whole tone below the octave.

Q For what reason is it called the Dominant 7th?

A Because it decides or governs the Tonic Harmony by containing those sounds which are not to be found in any other key or scale.

Q What is meant by a Fundamental Bass?

A Those notes are Fundamental which make the foundation of any certain chord.

Q What is a derived Bass?

A Those basses which derive their harmony from Fundamental notes.

Q Which are Major and which are Minor semitones?

A From C to C sharp is a Minor Semitone, and from C to D flat is a Major Semitone.

Q Whether is the Major or Minor Key the most perfect?

A The Major Key is perfect, but the Minor is imperfect, insomuch as it always wants the assistance of a sharp, or natural, as the case may be, to form its leading note.

THEORY OF MUSIC EXAMPLES

Common Chords

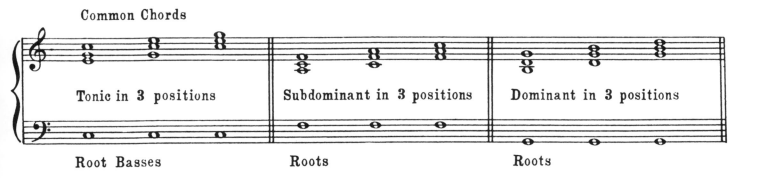

Tonic in **3** positions   Subdominant in **3** positions   Dominant in **3** positions

Root Basses   Roots   Roots

Chord of Dominant 7th

Derived Basses of the Common Chord
Chord of the 6th   Chord of the ⁶₄

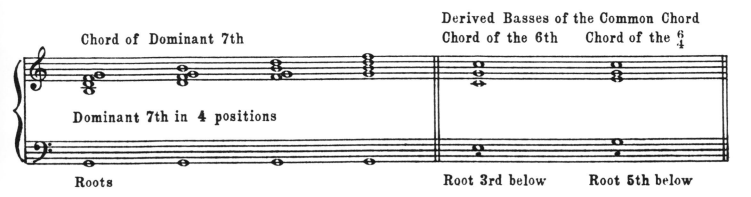

Dominant 7th in **4** positions

Roots   Root 3rd below   Root 5th below

Derived Basses of the Dominant 7th

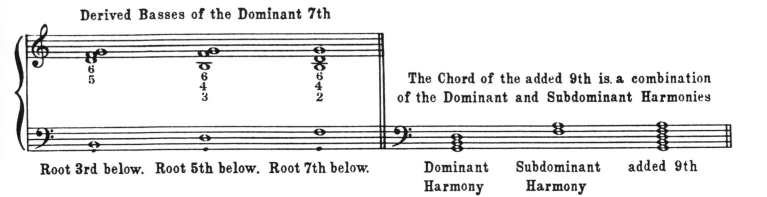

The Chord of the added 9th is a combination of the Dominant and Subdominant Harmonies

Root 3rd below. Root 5th below. Root 7th below.   Dominant Harmony   Subdominant Harmony   added 9th

The Major Scale harmonized introducing the Chords explained above.

This line shows the Roots of the Chords

DICTIONARY OF MUSICAL TERMS

Accelerando — gradually increasing the pace.

Adagio — very slow.

Affetuoso — tenderly.

Andante — rather slow.

Allegro — quick, cheerfully.

Allegretto — not so quick as Allegro.

Animato — with spirit.

Ad libitum or Ad lib. — at pleasure.

Brillante — in a brilliant, showy style.

Calando — **diminish the time and sound by** degrees.

Con spirito — **with quickness and spirit.**

Crescendo — **increasing the sound gradually.**

Cantabile — **in a graceful and singing style.**

Dolce — **sweetly, softly.**

Diminuendo — **diminishing the sound gradually.**

Da Capo or D.C. — **go back to the beginning.**

Deciso — **with decision, boldly.**

Espressivo — **with expression.**

Forte or f — **loud.**

Fortissimo or ff — **very loud.**

Furioso — **with fury.**

Forzando or fz — to mark well one **or more notes.**

Grave — slow, solemn.

Grazioso — in a flowing, **graceful style.**

Largo — a very slow movement.

Larghetto — not so slow as Largo.

Lento — in slow time.

Legato — **in a smooth connected manner.**

Loco — play the notes in the position in which they are written, and follows either of the signs *8va higher* or *8va bassa.*

Maestoso — **majestic**

Mezzo Forte or mf — rather loud.

Mezzo Piano or mp — rather soft.

Moderato — moderately quick.

Non troppo — not too much.

Presto — very quick.

Prestissimo — as quick as possible.

Piano, pia or p — soft.

Pianissimo or pp — very soft.

Poco — a little.

Poco a poco — little by little.

Pomposo — with dignity and grandeur.

Rallentando or Rall — gradually becoming slower.

Ritardando or Rit — retarding, delaying the tempo.

Risoluto — firmly, decided.

Scherzando — in a playful, light style.

Sforzando — see Forzando.

Sostenuto — to sustain every note to its full length.

Staccato — short and distinct.

Tema — a theme, or subject; a melody.

Tempo primo — time as at first.

Tenuto or ten — see Sostenuto.

Tremando — with a trembling effect.

Vigoroso — with strength and firmness.

Vivace — brisk and animated.

Volti Subito or V.S. — turn over quickly.

AFTER HOURS

Albums from Faber Music

PIANO

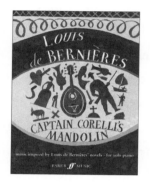

Captain Corelli's Mandolin *Richard Harris*

ISBN 0-571-52092-8

Cats (easy piano selection) *Andrew Lloyd Webber*

ISBN 0-571-50831-6

Children's Album *arranged by Daniel Scott*

ISBN 0-571-51103-1

The Faber Book of Showstoppers *arranged by Alan Gout*

ISBN 0-571-51063-9

The Faber Book of TV Themes *arranged by Alan Gout*

ISBN 0-571-51753-6

Great Film and TV Themes *Carl Davis*

ISBN 0-571-51740-4

Jane Austen's World *arranged by Richard Harris*

ISBN 0-571-51793-5

Shakespeare's World *arranged by Richard Harris*

ISBN 0-571-51907-5

The Snowman (easy piano suite) *Howard Blake*

ISBN 0-571-58044-0

FABER *ff* MUSIC